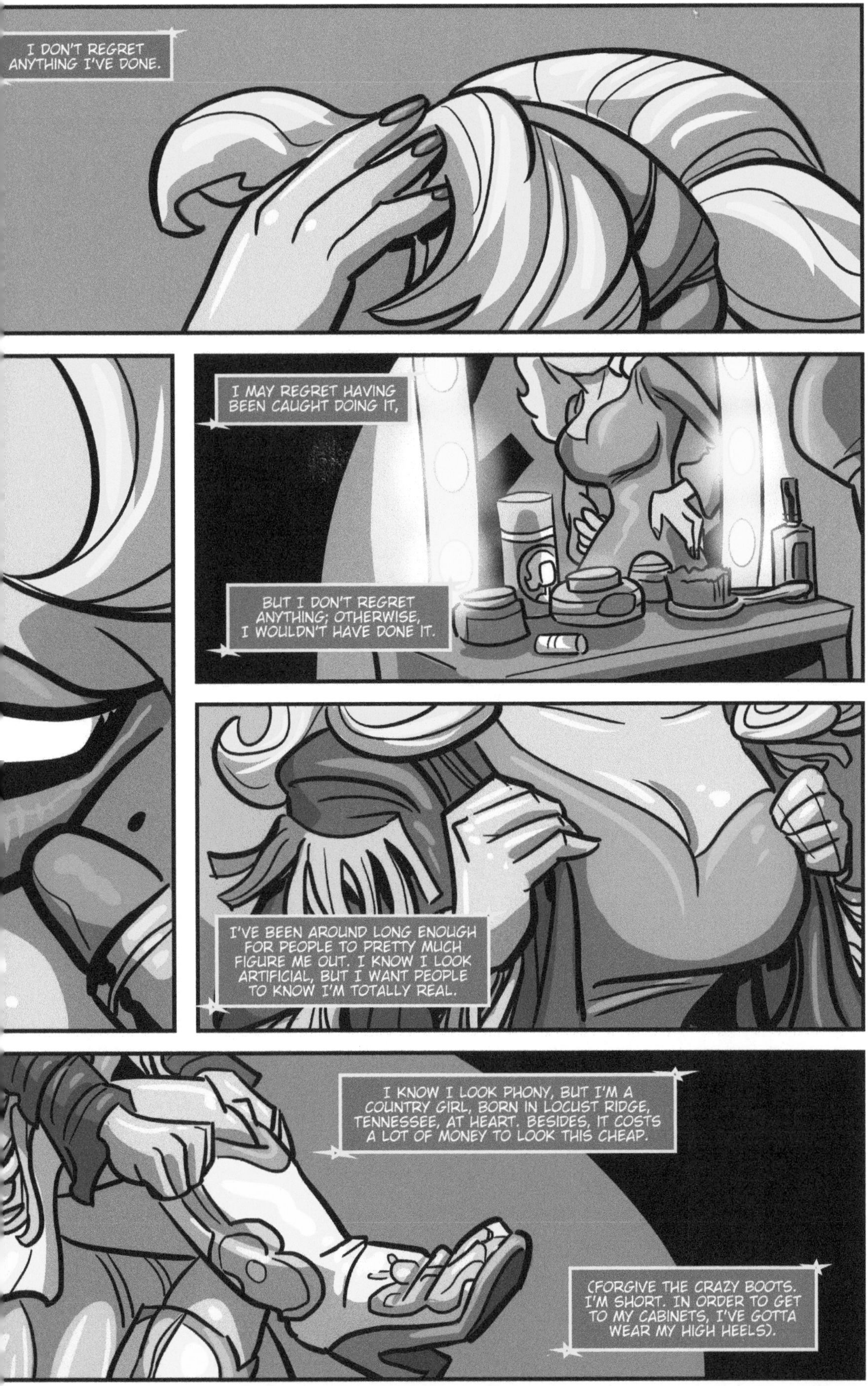
I DON'T REGRET ANYTHING I'VE DONE.
I MAY REGRET HAVING BEEN CAUGHT DOING IT,
BUT I DON'T REGRET ANYTHING; OTHERWISE, I WOULDN'T HAVE DONE IT.
I'VE BEEN AROUND LONG ENOUGH FOR PEOPLE TO PRETTY MUCH FIGURE ME OUT. I KNOW I LOOK ARTIFICIAL, BUT I WANT PEOPLE TO KNOW I'M TOTALLY REAL.
I KNOW I LOOK PHONY, BUT I'M A COUNTRY GIRL, BORN IN LOCUST RIDGE, TENNESSEE, AT HEART. BESIDES, IT COSTS A LOT OF MONEY TO LOOK THIS CHEAP.
(FORGIVE THE CRAZY BOOTS. I'M SHORT. IN ORDER TO GET TO MY CABINETS, I'VE GOTTA WEAR MY HIGH HEELS).

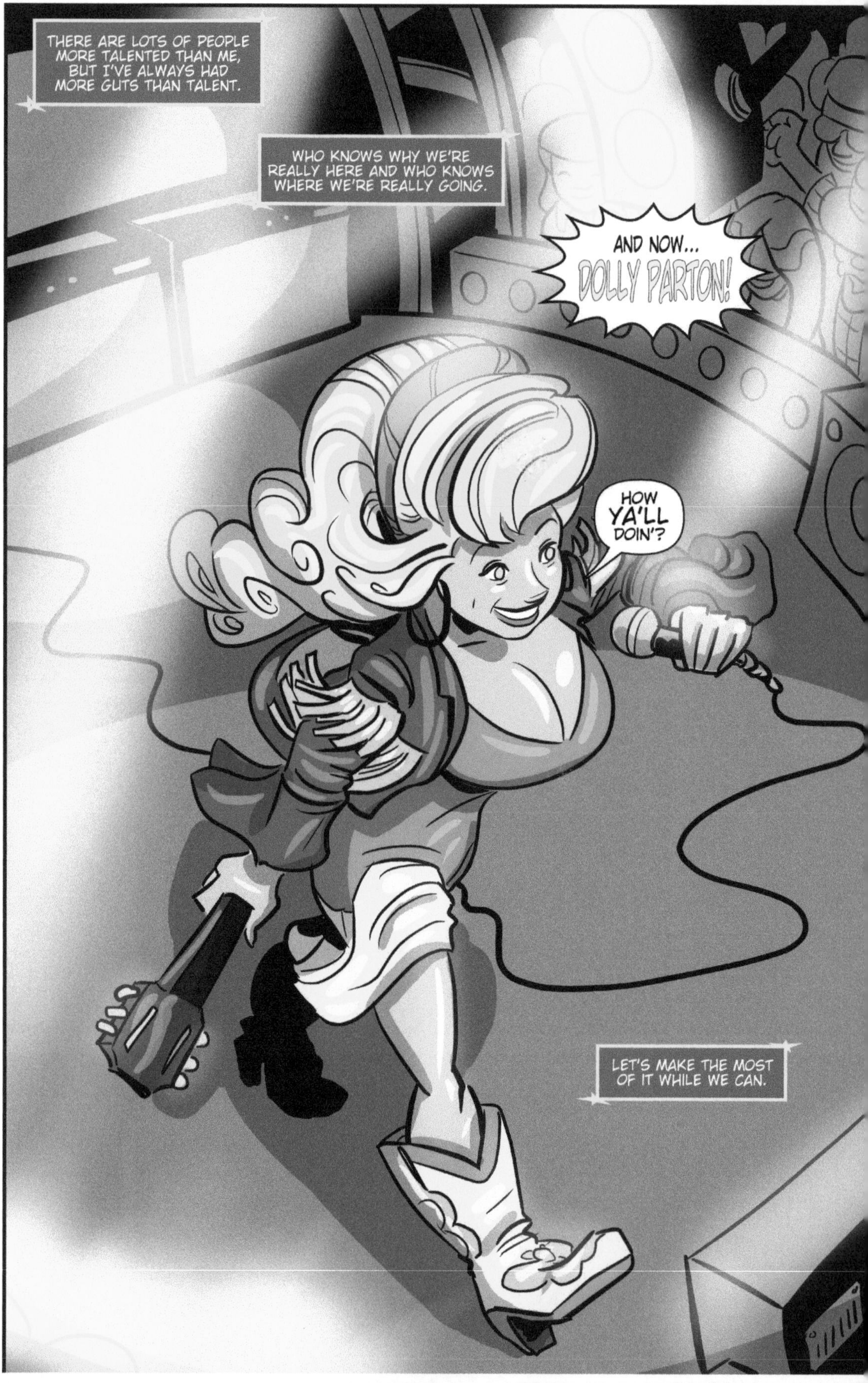
THERE ARE LOTS OF PEOPLE MORE TALENTED THAN ME, BUT I'VE ALWAYS HAD MORE GUTS THAN TALENT.
WHO KNOWS WHY WE'RE REALLY HERE AND WHO KNOWS WHERE WE'RE REALLY GOING.
AND NOW... DOLLY PARTON!
HOW YA'LL DOIN'?
LET'S MAKE THE MOST OF IT WHILE WE CAN.

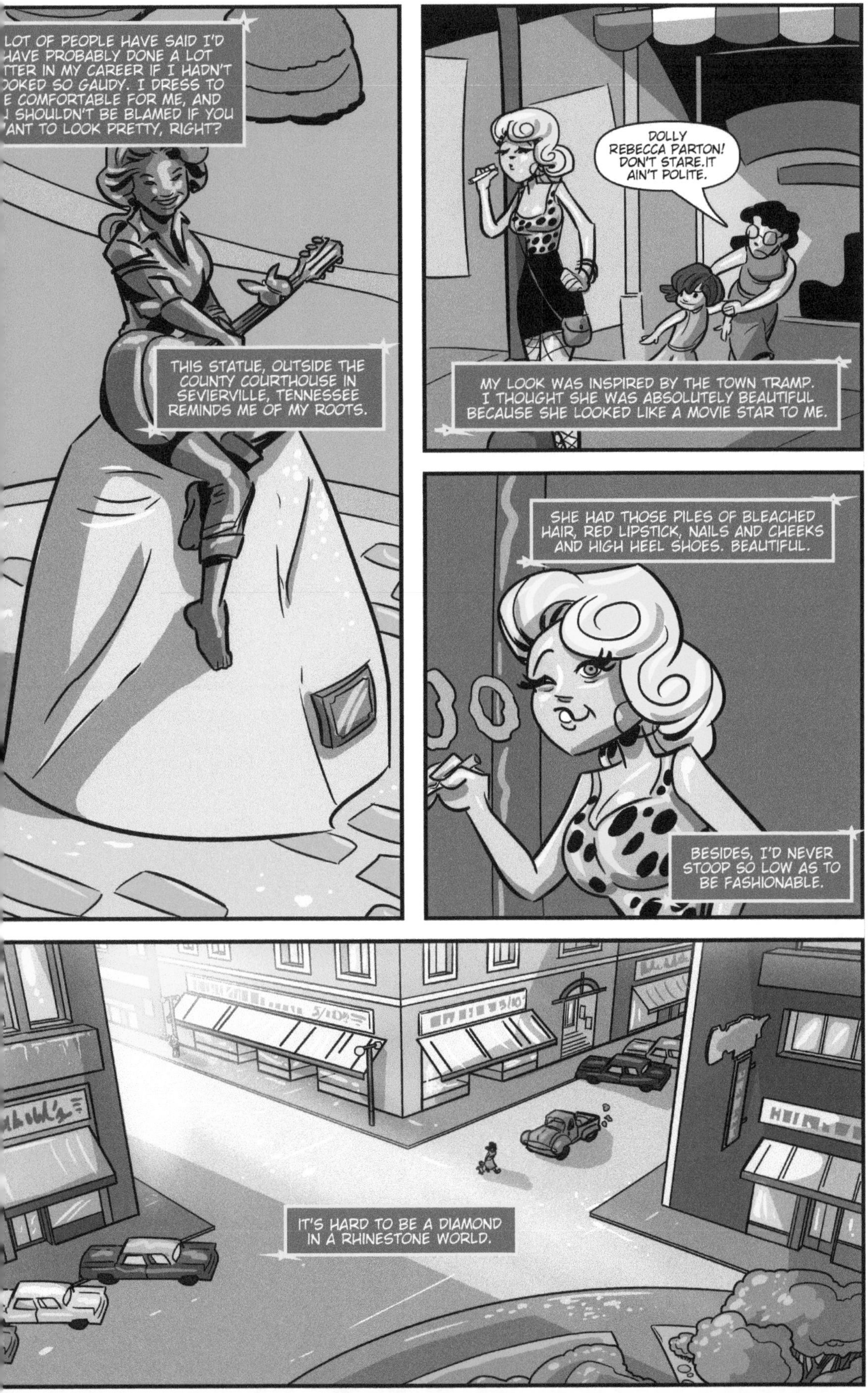
LOT OF PEOPLE HAVE SAID I'D HAVE PROBABLY DONE A LOT TTER IN MY CAREER IF I HADN'T OOKED SO GAUDY. I DRESS TO E COMFORTABLE FOR ME, AND I SHOULDN'T BE BLAMED IF YOU ANT TO LOOK PRETTY, RIGHT?
THIS STATUE, OUTSIDE THE COUNTY COURTHOUSE IN SEVIERVILLE, TENNESSEE REMINDS ME OF MY ROOTS.
DOLLY REBECCA PARTON! DON'T STARE.IT AIN'T POLITE.
MY LOOK WAS INSPIRED BY THE TOWN TRAMP. I THOUGHT SHE WAS ABSOLUTELY BEAUTIFUL BECAUSE SHE LOOKED LIKE A MOVIE STAR TO ME.
SHE HAD THOSE PILES OF BLEACHED HAIR, RED LIPSTICK, NAILS AND CHEEKS AND HIGH HEEL SHOES. BEAUTIFUL.
BESIDES, I'D NEVER STOOP SO LOW AS TO BE FASHIONABLE.
IT'S HARD TO BE A DIAMOND IN A RHINESTONE WORLD.

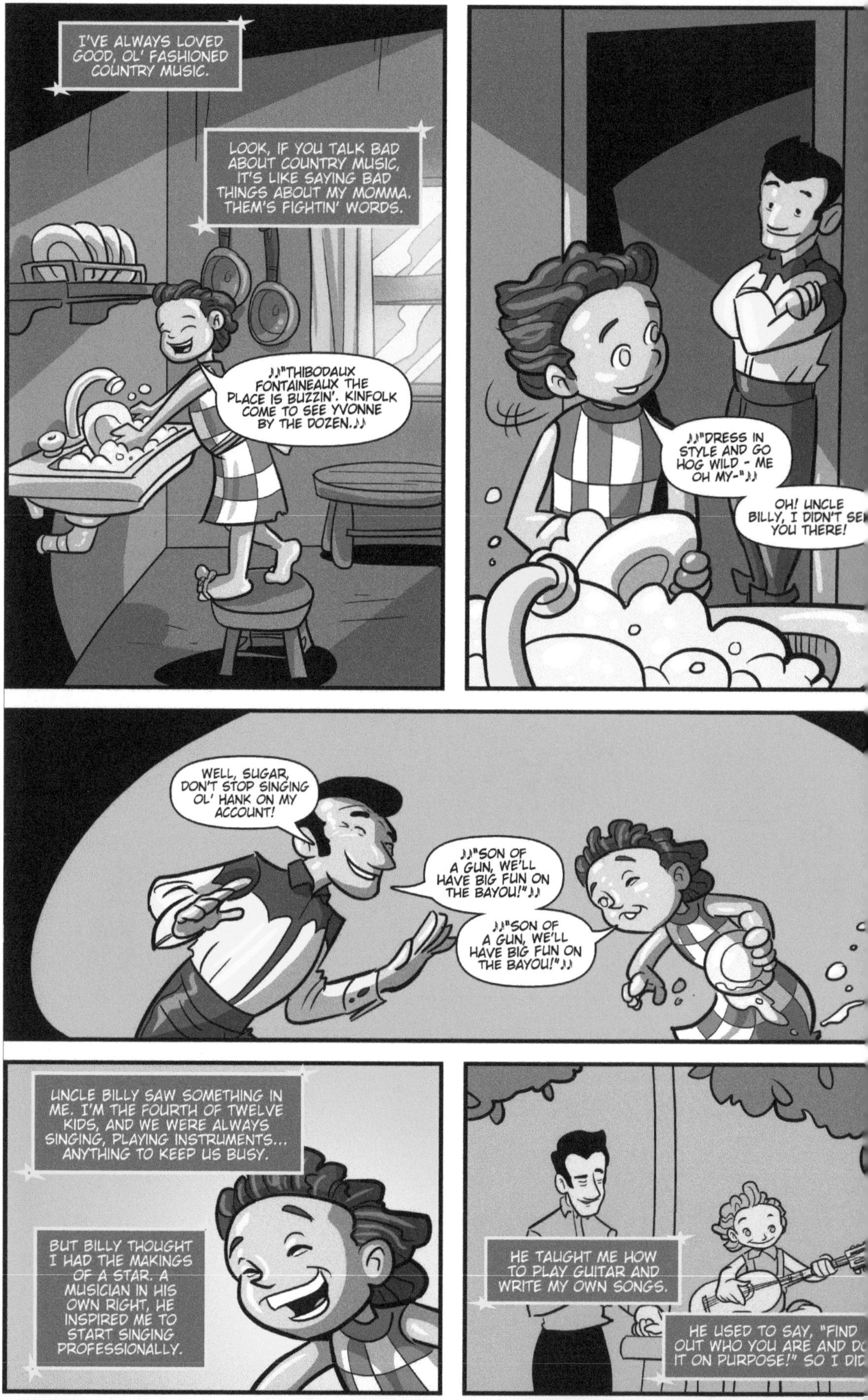

I'VE ALWAYS LOVED GOOD, OL' FASHIONED COUNTRY MUSIC.
LOOK, IF YOU TALK BAD ABOUT COUNTRY MUSIC, IT'S LIKE SAYING BAD THINGS ABOUT MY MOMMA. THEM'S FIGHTIN' WORDS.
♪♪"THIBODAUX FONTAINEAUX THE PLACE IS BUZZIN'. KINFOLK COME TO SEE YVONNE BY THE DOZEN.♪♪
♪♪"DRESS IN STYLE AND GO HOG WILD - ME OH MY-"♪♪
OH! UNCLE BILLY, I DIDN'T SE
YOU THERE!
WELL, SUGAR, DON'T STOP SINGING OL' HANK ON MY ACCOUNT!
♪♪"SON OF A GUN, WE'LL HAVE BIG FUN ON THE BAYOU!"♪♪
♪♪"SON OF A GUN, WE'LL HAVE BIG FUN ON THE BAYOU!"♪♪
UNCLE BILLY SAW SOMETHING IN ME. I'M THE FOURTH OF TWELVE KIDS, AND WE WERE ALWAYS SINGING, PLAYING INSTRUMENTS... ANYTHING TO KEEP US BUSY.
BUT BILLY THOUGHT I HAD THE MAKINGS OF A STAR. A MUSICIAN IN HIS OWN RIGHT, HE INSPIRED ME TO START SINGING PROFESSIONALLY.
HE TAUGHT ME HOW TO PLAY GUITAR AND WRITE MY OWN SONGS.
HE USED TO SAY, "FIND OUT WHO YOU ARE AND D
IT ON PURPOSE!" SO I DI

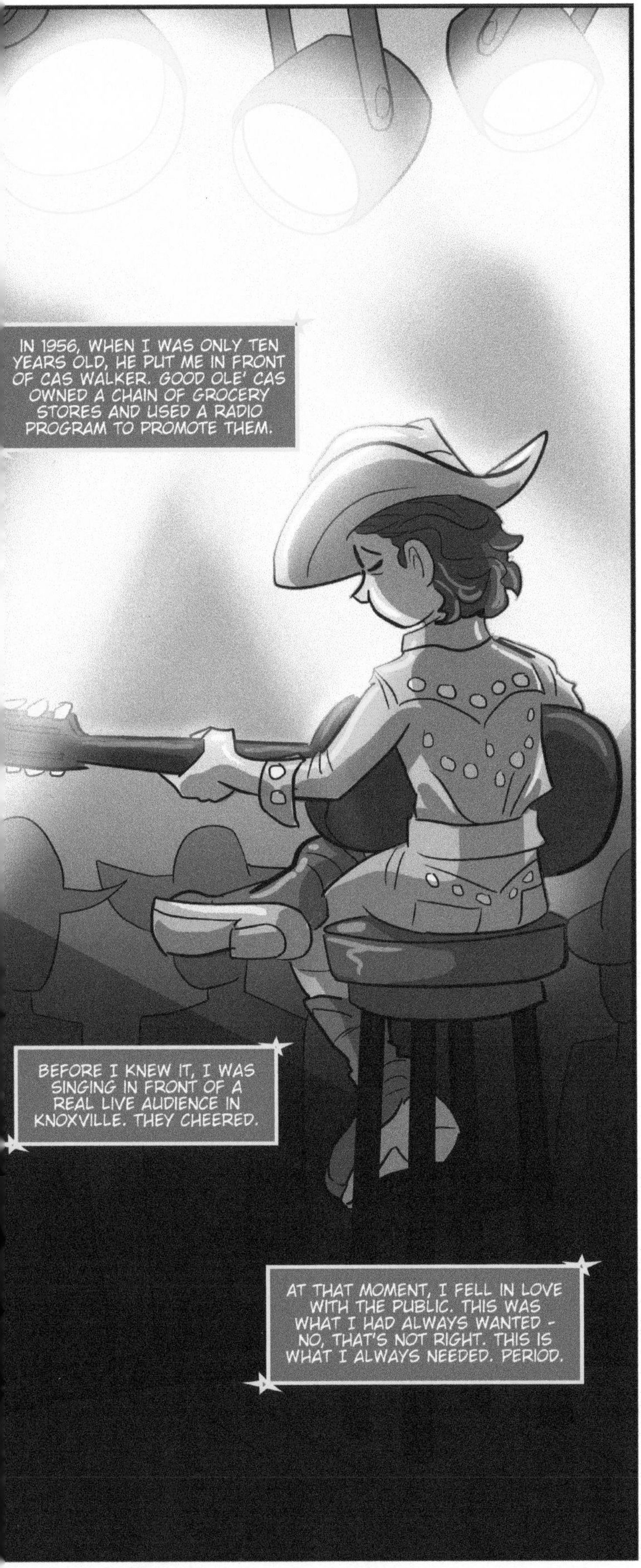
IN 1956, WHEN I WAS ONLY TEN YEARS OLD, HE PUT ME IN FRONT OF CAS WALKER. GOOD OLE' CAS OWNED A CHAIN OF GROCERY STORES AND USED A RADIO PROGRAM TO PROMOTE THEM.
BEFORE I KNEW IT, I WAS SINGING IN FRONT OF A REAL LIVE AUDIENCE IN KNOXVILLE. THEY CHEERED.
AT THAT MOMENT, I FELL IN LOVE WITH THE PUBLIC. THIS WAS WHAT I HAD ALWAYS WANTED - NO, THAT'S NOT RIGHT. THIS IS WHAT I ALWAYS NEEDED. PERIOD.
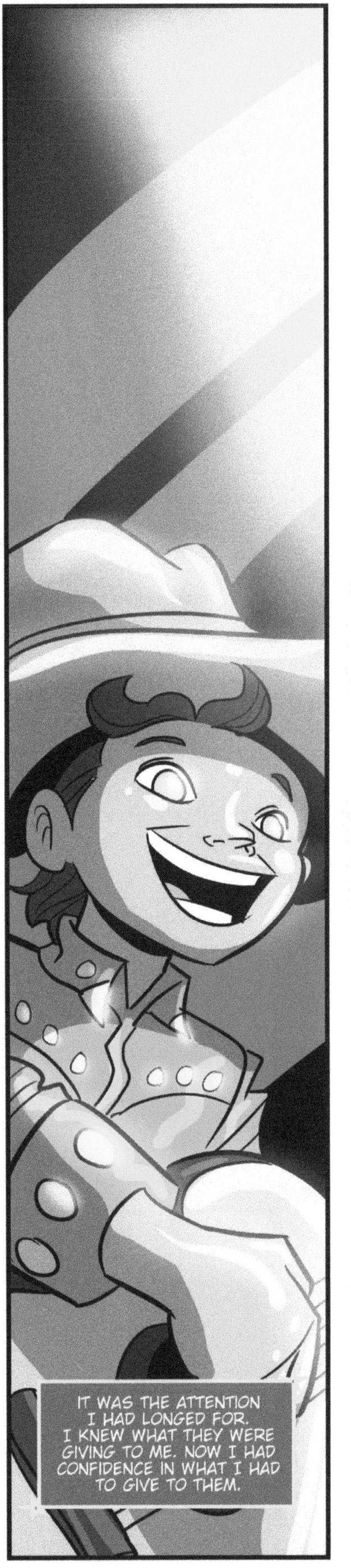
IT WAS THE ATTENTION I HAD LONGED FOR. I KNEW WHAT THEY WERE GIVING TO ME. NOW I HAD CONFIDENCE IN WHAT I HAD TO GIVE TO THEM.

YOU NEED TO REALLY BELIEVE IN WHAT YOU'VE GOT TO OFFER, WHAT YOUR TALENT IS — AND IF YOU BELIEVE, THAT GIVES YOU STRENGTH.

SO UNCLE BILLY AND I STARTED KNOCKING ON DOORS AND CALLING IN FAVORS. BY THE TIME I WAS TWELVE, I APPEARED ON THE GRAND OLE OPRY THANKS TO SINGER AND SONGWRITER JIMMY C. NEWMAN. THAT CRAZY CAJUN GAVE ME HIS SPOT ON THE SHOW!

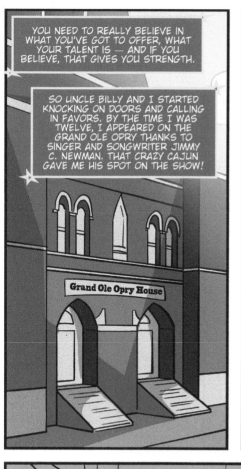

Grand Ole Opry House

BUT I WANTED MORE. WHEN I WAS SIXTEEN, UNCLE BILLY BROUGHT ME TO THE OFFICES OF TREE PUBLISHING.

WE'RE HERE TO SEE YOUR –

HE'S OUT.

NOW, WHO DID YOU THINK I –

YOU DON'T HAVE AN APPOINTMENT.

"FINE. WE'LL WAIT."

AND WE DID. ALL DAY. I THINK THEY FINALLY SAW US BECAUSE THEY WANTED TO CLOSE THE OFFICE.

THAT EVENING, UNCLE BILLY AND I SIGNED A DEAL WITH MERCURY RECORDS AND I RECORDED "IT MAY NOT KILL ME (BUT IT'S SURE GONNA HURT)" AND "I WASTED MY TEARS (WHEN I CRIED OVER YOU.)"

IF YOU HAVEN'T HAD THIS EXPERIENCE, LET ME TELL YA, IT'S A WARM FEELIN' TO HEAR YOUR MUSIC ON THE RADIO.

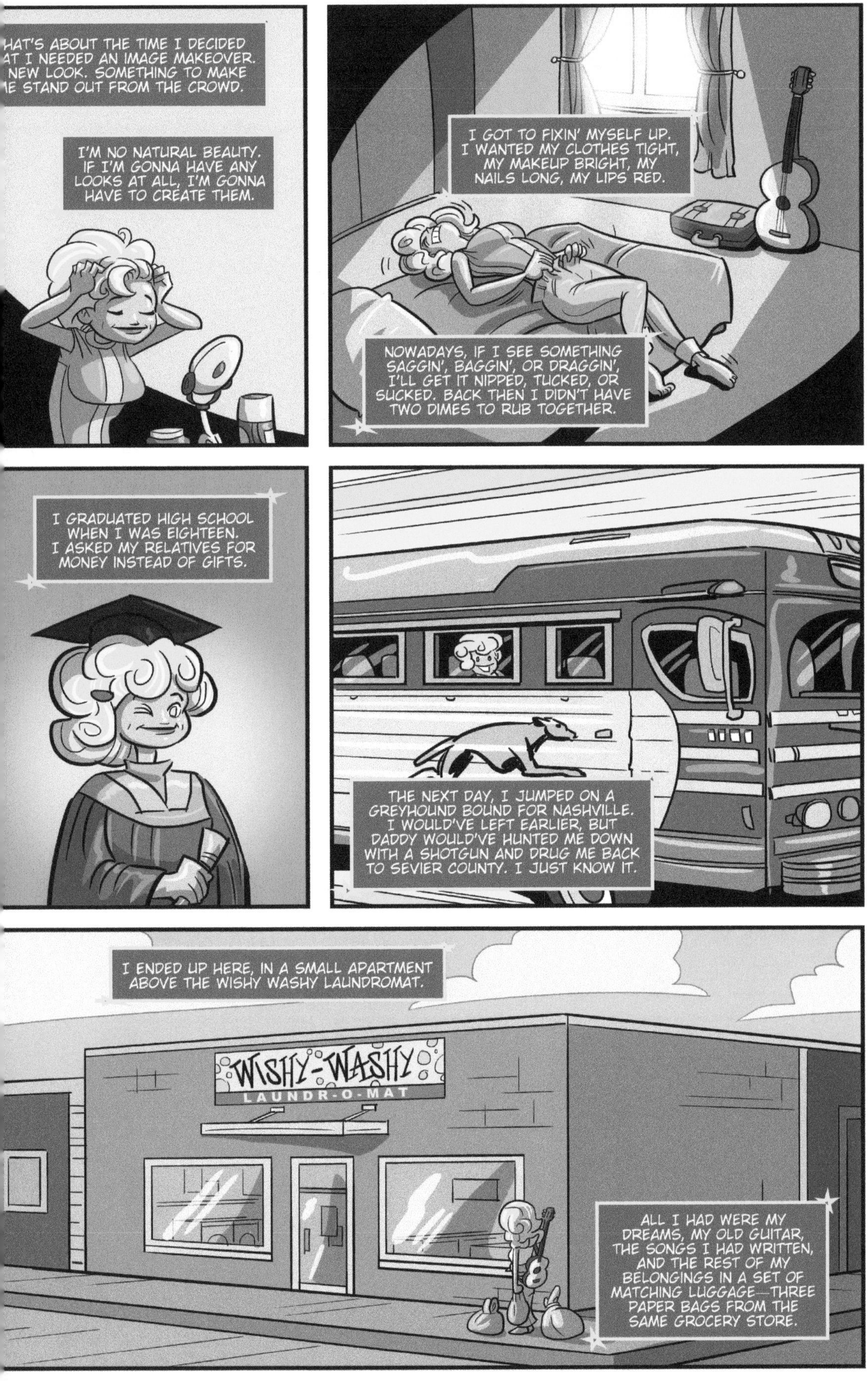
HAT'S ABOUT THE TIME I DECIDED
AT I NEEDED AN IMAGE MAKEOVER.
NEW LOOK. SOMETHING TO MAKE
IE STAND OUT FROM THE CROWD.
I'M NO NATURAL BEAUTY. IF I'M GONNA HAVE ANY LOOKS AT ALL, I'M GONNA HAVE TO CREATE THEM.
I GOT TO FIXIN' MYSELF UP. I WANTED MY CLOTHES TIGHT, MY MAKEUP BRIGHT, MY NAILS LONG, MY LIPS RED.
NOWADAYS, IF I SEE SOMETHING SAGGIN', BAGGIN', OR DRAGGIN', I'LL GET IT NIPPED, TUCKED, OR SUCKED. BACK THEN I DIDN'T HAVE TWO DIMES TO RUB TOGETHER.
I GRADUATED HIGH SCHOOL WHEN I WAS EIGHTEEN. I ASKED MY RELATIVES FOR MONEY INSTEAD OF GIFTS.
THE NEXT DAY, I JUMPED ON A GREYHOUND BOUND FOR NASHVILLE. I WOULD'VE LEFT EARLIER, BUT DADDY WOULD'VE HUNTED ME DOWN WITH A SHOTGUN AND DRUG ME BACK TO SEVIER COUNTY. I JUST KNOW IT.
I ENDED UP HERE, IN A SMALL APARTMENT ABOVE THE WISHY WASHY LAUNDROMAT.
WISHY-WASHY
LAUNDR-O-MAT
ALL I HAD WERE MY DREAMS, MY OLD GUITAR, THE SONGS I HAD WRITTEN, AND THE REST OF MY BELONGINGS IN A SET OF MATCHING LUGGAGE—THREE PAPER BAGS FROM THE SAME GROCERY STORE.

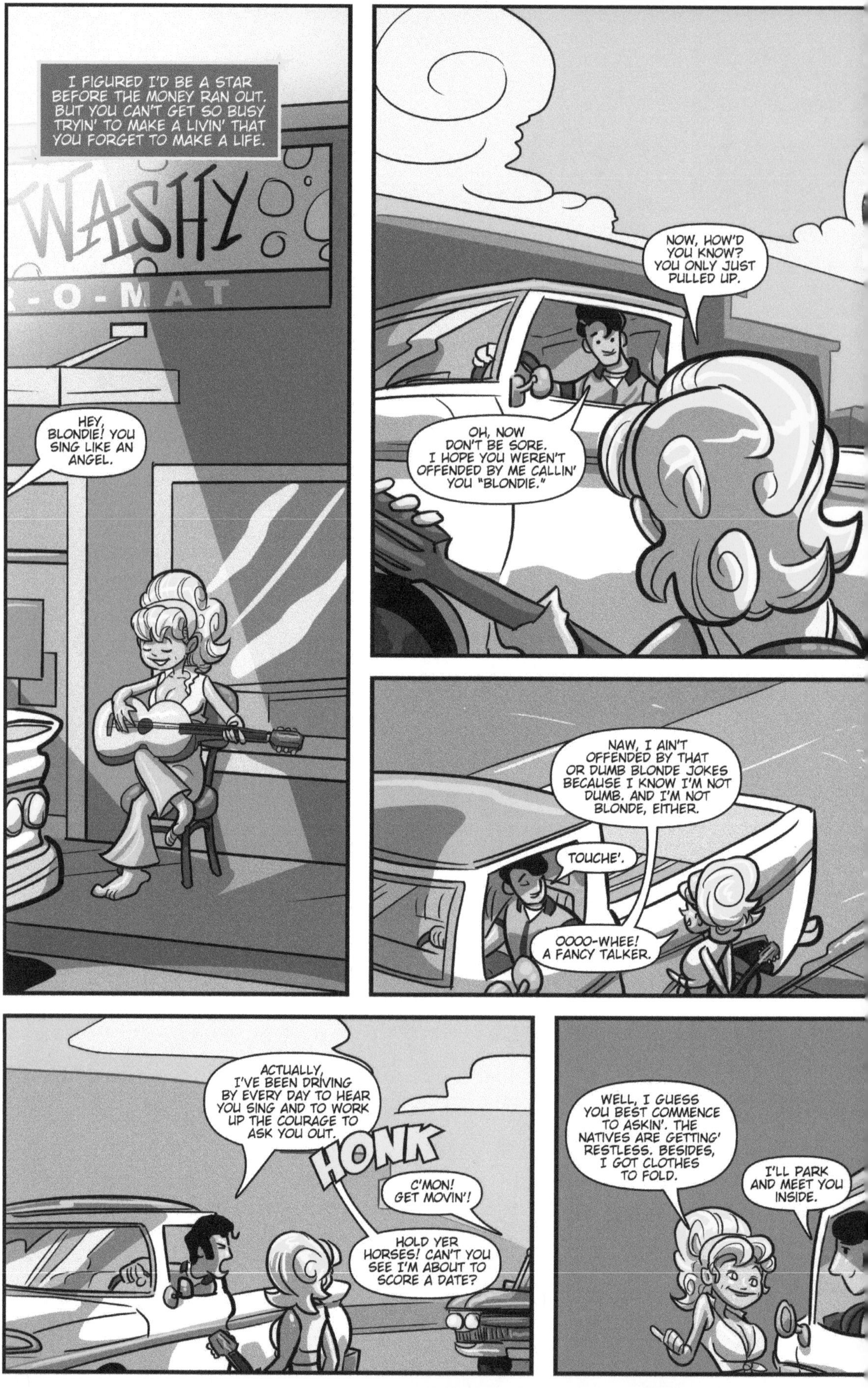
I FIGURED I'D BE A STAR BEFORE THE MONEY RAN OUT. BUT YOU CAN'T GET SO BUSY TRYIN' TO MAKE A LIVIN' THAT YOU FORGET TO MAKE A LIFE.
WASHY
R-O-MAT
HEY, BLONDIE! YOU SING LIKE AN ANGEL.
NOW, HOW'D YOU KNOW? YOU ONLY JUST PULLED UP.
OH, NOW DON'T BE SORE. I HOPE YOU WEREN'T OFFENDED BY ME CALLIN' YOU "BLONDIE."
NAW, I AIN'T OFFENDED BY THAT OR DUMB BLONDE JOKES BECAUSE I KNOW I'M NOT DUMB. AND I'M NOT BLONDE, EITHER.
TOUCHE'.
OOOO-WHEE! A FANCY TALKER.
ACTUALLY, I'VE BEEN DRIVING BY EVERY DAY TO HEAR YOU SING AND TO WORK UP THE COURAGE TO ASK YOU OUT.
HONK
C'MON! GET MOVIN'!
HOLD YER HORSES! CAN'T YOU SEE I'M ABOUT TO SCORE A DATE?
WELL, I GUESS YOU BEST COMMENCE TO ASKIN'. THE NATIVES ARE GETTING' RESTLESS. BESIDES, I GOT CLOTHES TO FOLD.
I'LL PARK AND MEET YOU INSIDE.

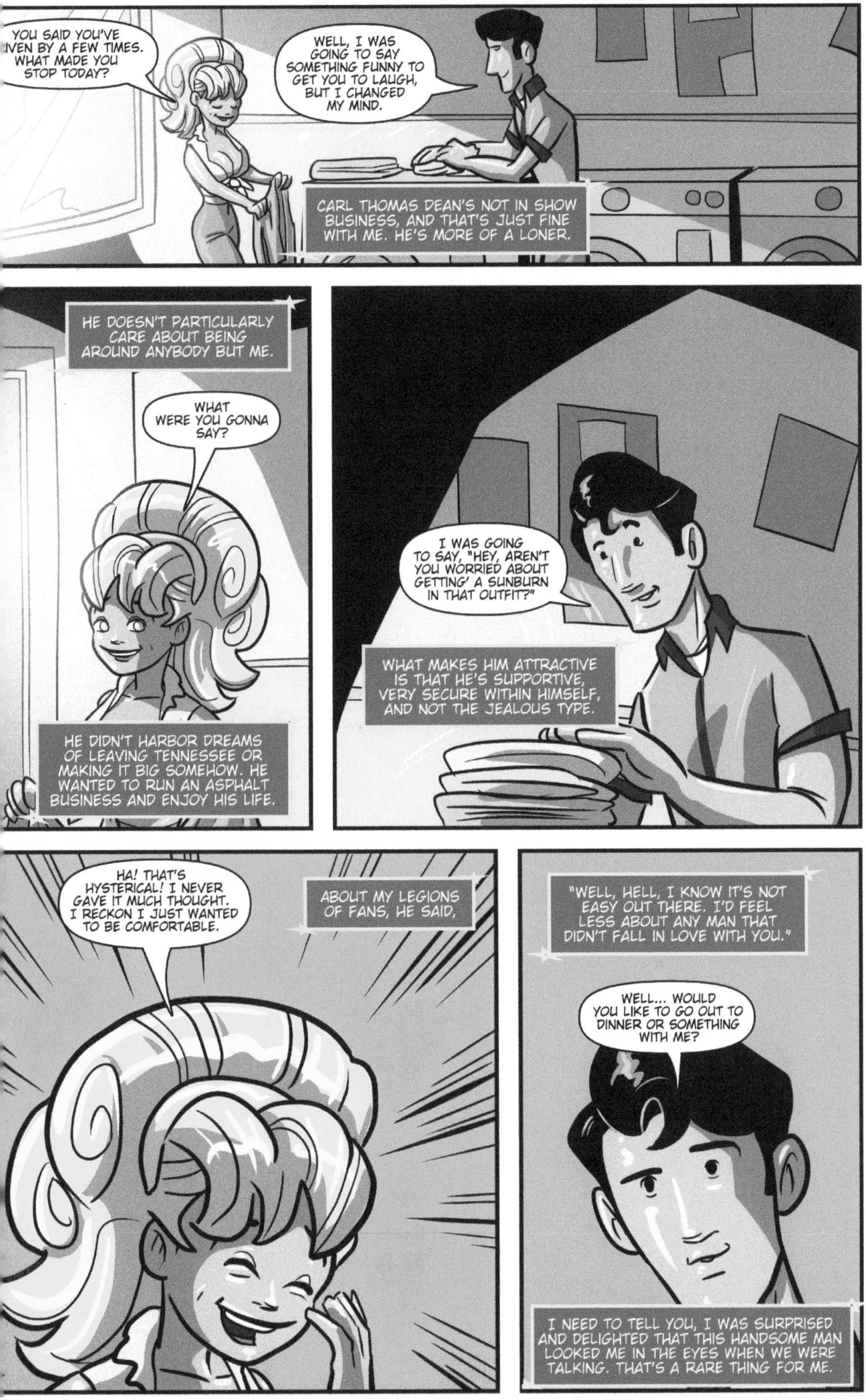
YOU SAID YOU'VE
RIVEN BY A FEW TIMES. WHAT MADE YOU STOP TODAY?
WELL, I WAS GOING TO SAY SOMETHING FUNNY TO GET YOU TO LAUGH, BUT I CHANGED MY MIND.
CARL THOMAS DEAN'S NOT IN SHOW BUSINESS, AND THAT'S JUST FINE WITH ME. HE'S MORE OF A LONER.
HE DOESN'T PARTICULARLY CARE ABOUT BEING AROUND ANYBODY BUT ME.
WHAT WERE YOU GONNA SAY?
HE DIDN'T HARBOR DREAMS OF LEAVING TENNESSEE OR MAKING IT BIG SOMEHOW. HE WANTED TO RUN AN ASPHALT BUSINESS AND ENJOY HIS LIFE.
I WAS GOING TO SAY, "HEY, AREN'T YOU WORRIED ABOUT GETTING' A SUNBURN IN THAT OUTFIT?"
WHAT MAKES HIM ATTRACTIVE IS THAT HE'S SUPPORTIVE, VERY SECURE WITHIN HIMSELF, AND NOT THE JEALOUS TYPE.
HA! THAT'S HYSTERICAL! I NEVER GAVE IT MUCH THOUGHT. I RECKON I JUST WANTED TO BE COMFORTABLE.
ABOUT MY LEGIONS OF FANS, HE SAID,
"WELL, HELL, I KNOW IT'S NOT EASY OUT THERE. I'D FEEL LESS ABOUT ANY MAN THAT DIDN'T FALL IN LOVE WITH YOU."
WELL... WOULD YOU LIKE TO GO OUT TO DINNER OR SOMETHING WITH ME?
I NEED TO TELL YOU, I WAS SURPRISED AND DELIGHTED THAT THIS HANDSOME MAN LOOKED ME IN THE EYES WHEN WE WERE TALKING. THAT'S A RARE THING FOR ME.

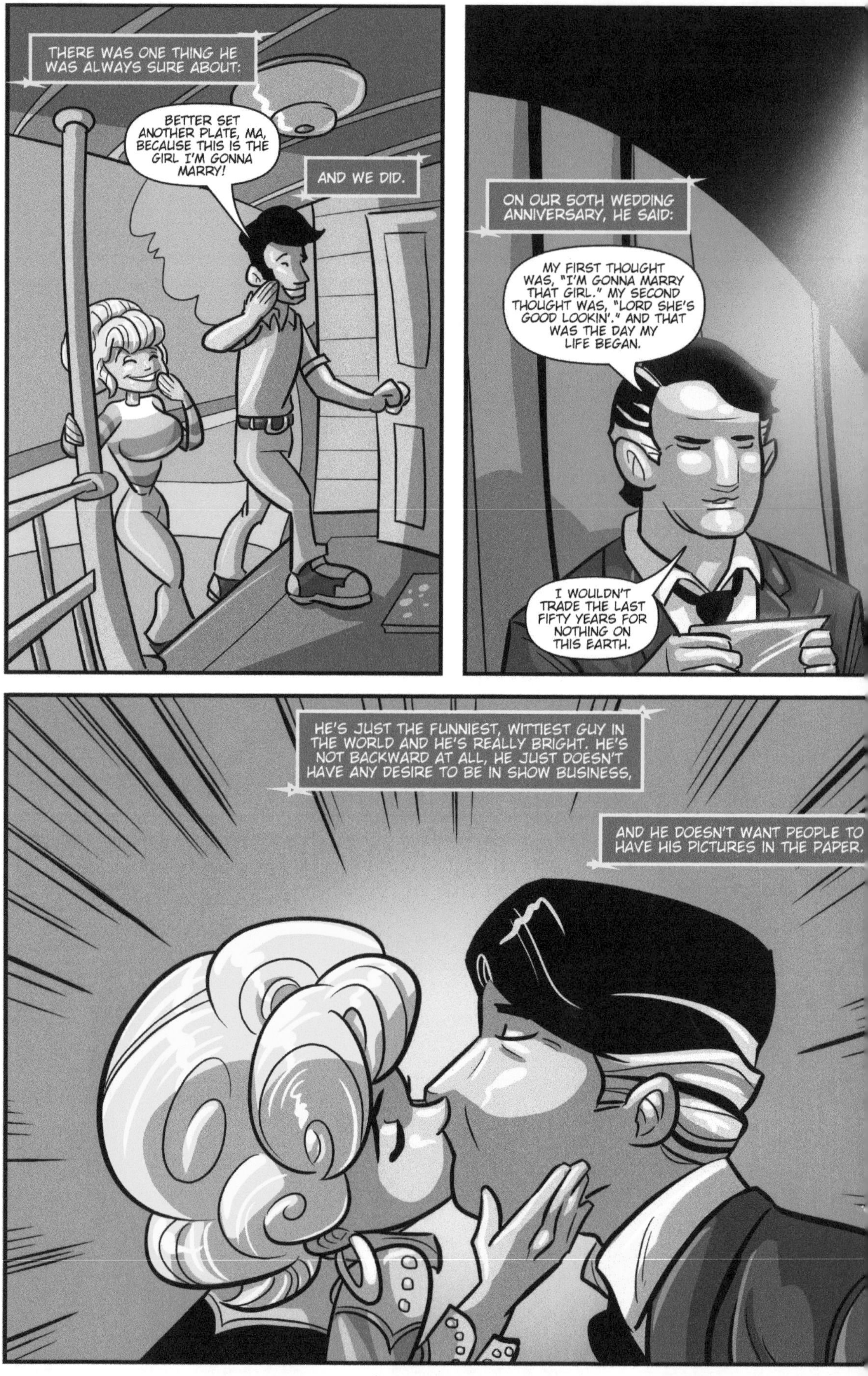
THERE WAS ONE THING HE WAS ALWAYS SURE ABOUT:
BETTER SET ANOTHER PLATE, MA, BECAUSE THIS IS THE GIRL I'M GONNA MARRY!
AND WE DID.
ON OUR 50TH WEDDING ANNIVERSARY, HE SAID:
MY FIRST THOUGHT WAS, "I'M GONNA MARRY THAT GIRL." MY SECOND THOUGHT WAS, "LORD SHE'S GOOD LOOKIN'." AND THAT WAS THE DAY MY LIFE BEGAN.
I WOULDN'T TRADE THE LAST FIFTY YEARS FOR NOTHING ON THIS EARTH.
HE'S JUST THE FUNNIEST, WITTIEST GUY IN THE WORLD AND HE'S REALLY BRIGHT. HE'S NOT BACKWARD AT ALL, HE JUST DOESN'T HAVE ANY DESIRE TO BE IN SHOW BUSINESS,
AND HE DOESN'T WANT PEOPLE TO HAVE HIS PICTURES IN THE PAPER.

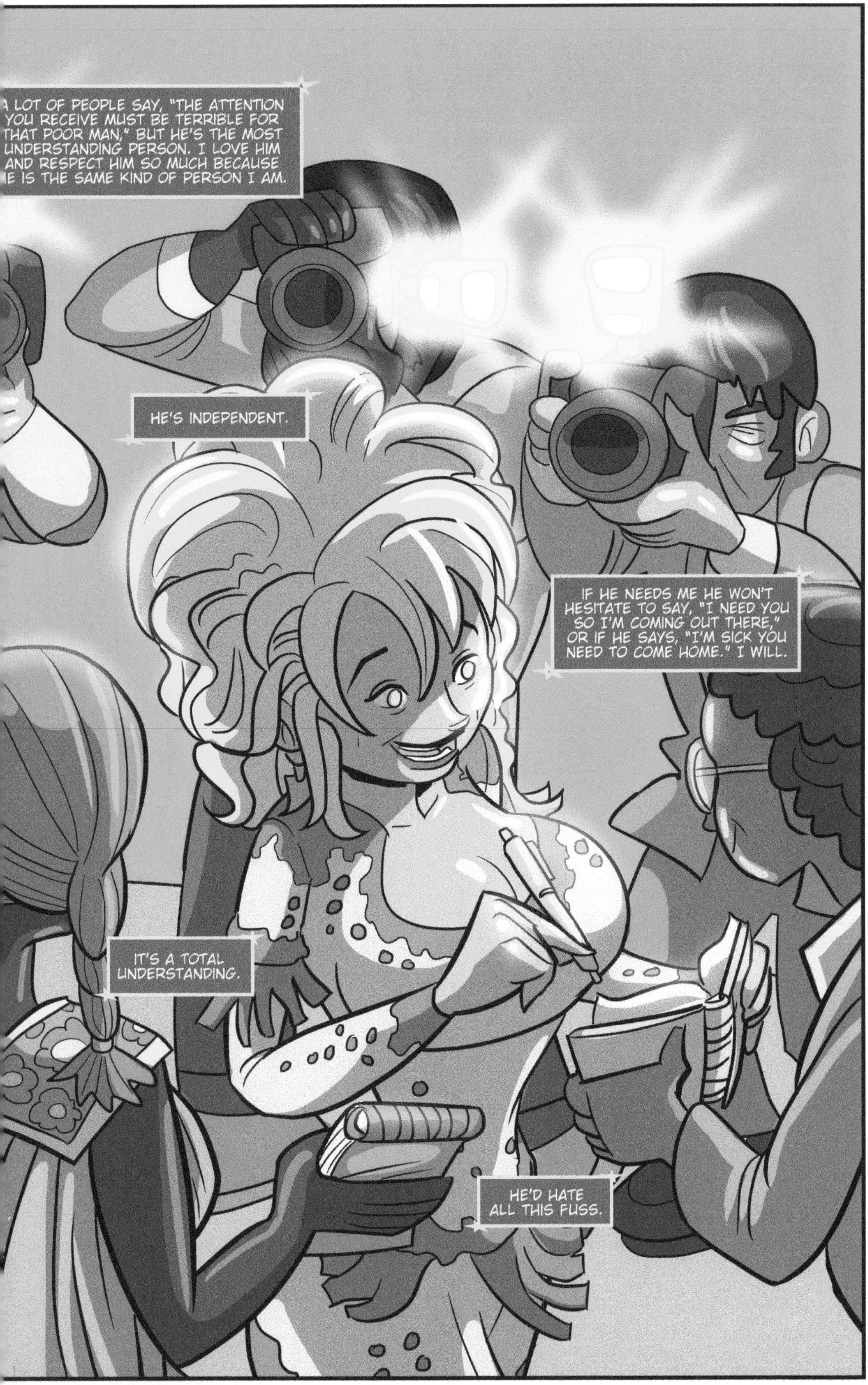
A LOT OF PEOPLE SAY, "THE ATTENTION YOU RECEIVE MUST BE TERRIBLE FOR THAT POOR MAN," BUT HE'S THE MOST UNDERSTANDING PERSON. I LOVE HIM AND RESPECT HIM SO MUCH BECAUSE E IS THE SAME KIND OF PERSON I AM.
HE'S INDEPENDENT.
IF HE NEEDS ME HE WON'T HESITATE TO SAY, "I NEED YOU SO I'M COMING OUT THERE," OR IF HE SAYS, "I'M SICK YOU NEED TO COME HOME." I WILL.
IT'S A TOTAL UNDERSTANDING.
HE'D HATE ALL THIS FUSS.

IN MY WILDEST DREAMS, I DIDN'T EXPECT THINGS TO TAKE OFF LIKE THEY DID. IT REALLY STARTED WHEN I MET PORTER WAGONER.

I REMEMBER HUDDLING IN FRONT OF THE TELEVISION TO WATCH THE PORTER WAGONER SHOW.

PORTER, "THE THIN MAN FROM WEST PLAINS, MISSOURI," HAD 29 TOP-TEN HITS DURING HIS CAREER, INCLUDING "MISERY LOVES COMPANY" AND "THE COLD HARD FACTS OF LIFE."

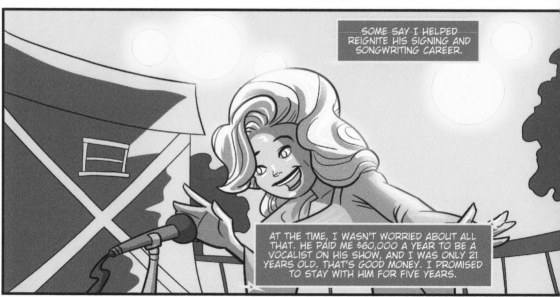

SOME SAY I HELPED REIGNITE HIS SIGNING AND SONGWRITING CAREER.

AT THE TIME, I WASN'T WORRIED ABOUT ALL THAT. HE PAID ME $60,000 A YEAR TO BE A VOCALIST ON HIS SHOW, AND I WAS ONLY 21 YEARS OLD. THAT'S GOOD MONEY. I PROMISED TO STAY WITH HIM FOR FIVE YEARS.

WE HAD 21 HITS TOP THE CHARTS TOGETHER AND WON THE COUNTRY MUSIC ASSOCIATION'S VOCAL DUO OF THE YEAR AWARD THREE TIMES.

BUT I ALWAYS SAY, "IF YOU DON'T LIKE THE ROAD YOU'RE WALKING ON, PAVE ANOTHER."

I KNEW IT WAS TIME TO BE ON MY OWN. I WANTED MORE. I WANTED HOLLYWOOD.

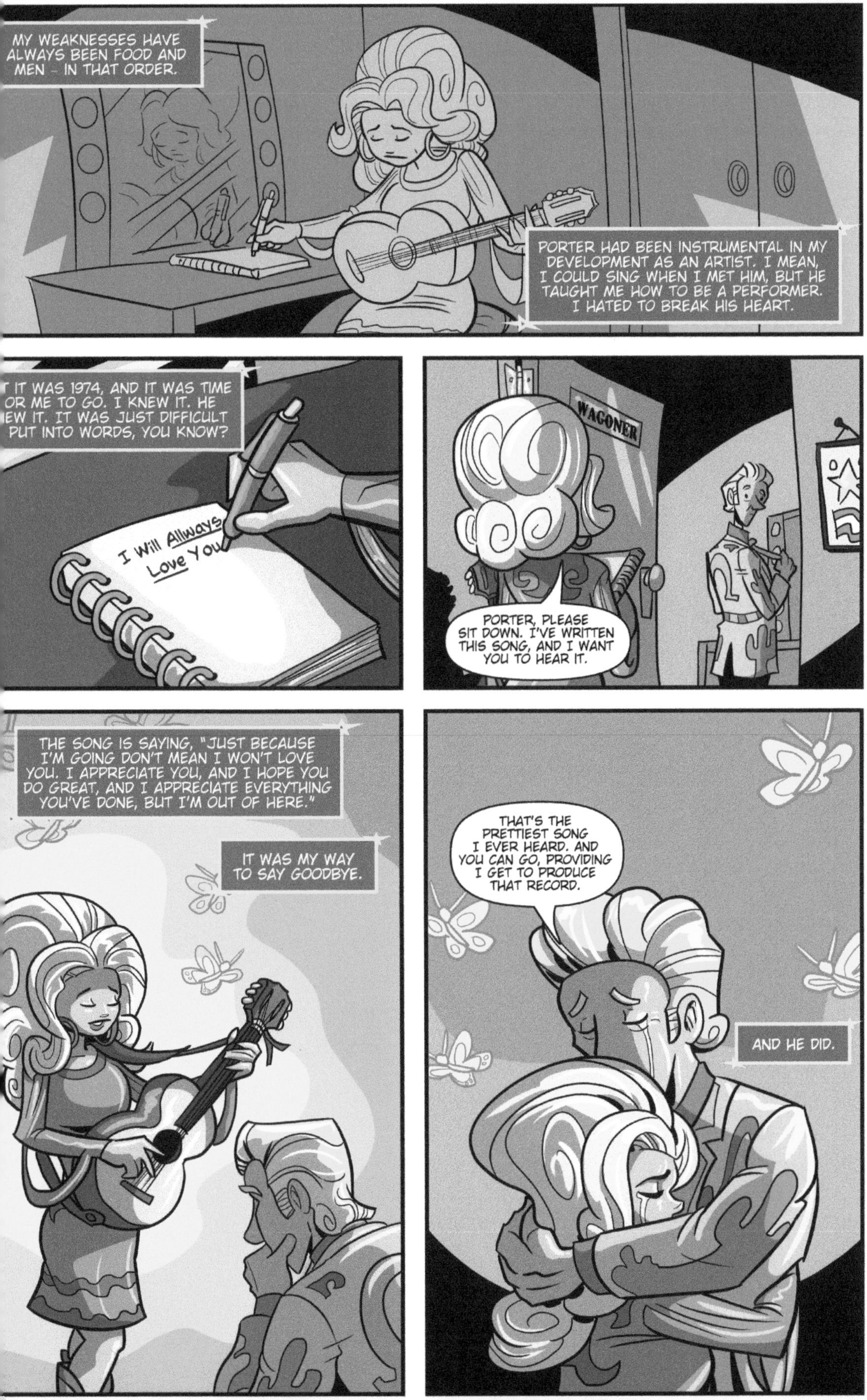
MY WEAKNESSES HAVE ALWAYS BEEN FOOD AND MEN - IN THAT ORDER.
PORTER HAD BEEN INSTRUMENTAL IN MY DEVELOPMENT AS AN ARTIST. I MEAN, I COULD SING WHEN I MET HIM, BUT HE TAUGHT ME HOW TO BE A PERFORMER. I HATED TO BREAK HIS HEART.
IT WAS 1974, AND IT WAS TIME OR ME TO GO. I KNEW IT. HE EW IT. IT WAS JUST DIFFICULT PUT INTO WORDS, YOU KNOW?
I Will Always Love You
WAGONER
PORTER, PLEASE SIT DOWN. I'VE WRITTEN THIS SONG, AND I WANT YOU TO HEAR IT.
THE SONG IS SAYING, "JUST BECAUSE I'M GOING DON'T MEAN I WON'T LOVE YOU. I APPRECIATE YOU, AND I HOPE YOU DO GREAT, AND I APPRECIATE EVERYTHING YOU'VE DONE, BUT I'M OUT OF HERE."
IT WAS MY WAY TO SAY GOODBYE.
THAT'S THE PRETTIEST SONG I EVER HEARD. AND YOU CAN GO, PROVIDING I GET TO PRODUCE THAT RECORD.
AND HE DID.

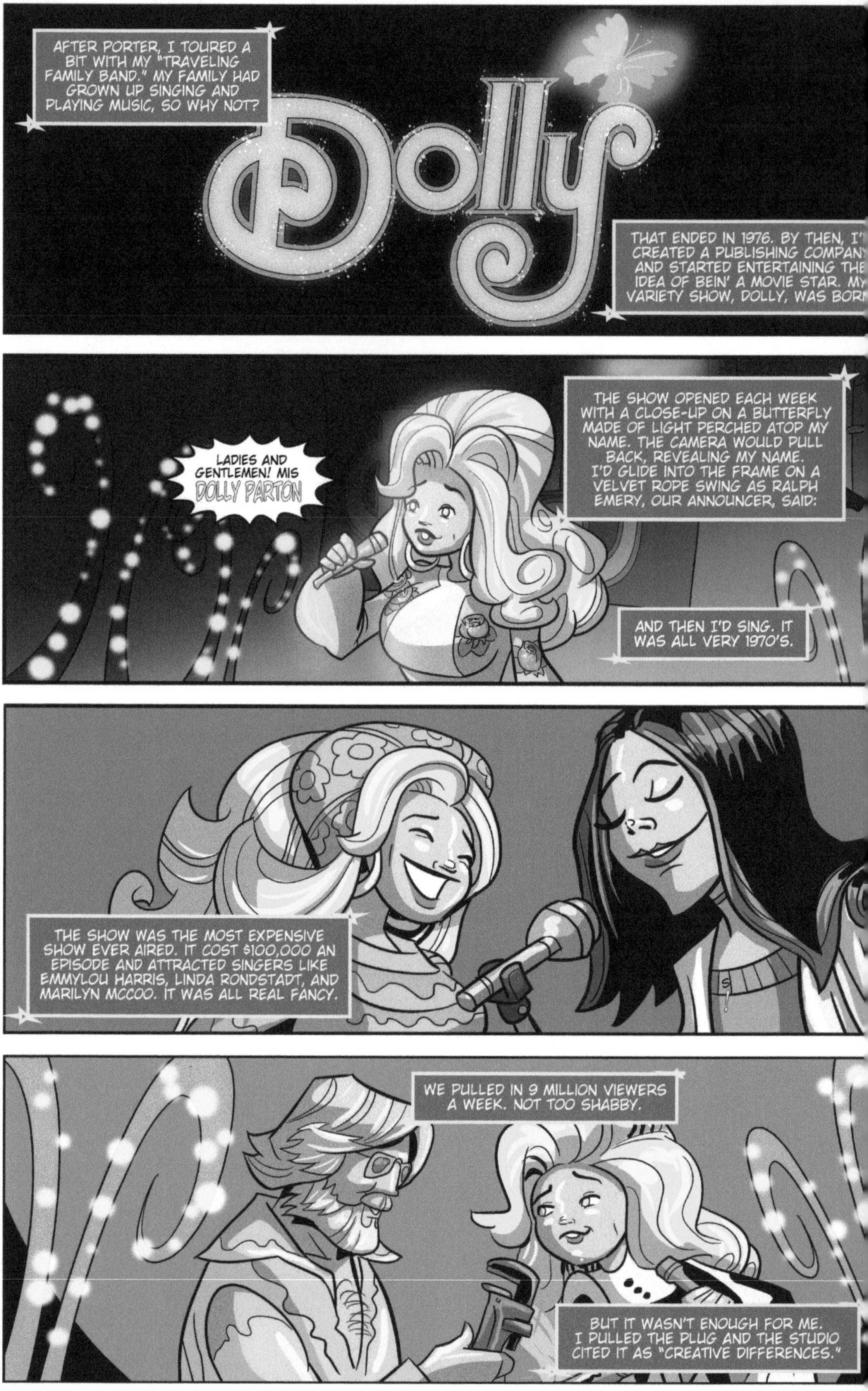

AFTER PORTER, I TOURED A BIT WITH MY "TRAVELING FAMILY BAND." MY FAMILY HAD GROWN UP SINGING AND PLAYING MUSIC, SO WHY NOT?
Dolly
THAT ENDED IN 1976. BY THEN, I'
CREATED A PUBLISHING COMPAN
AND STARTED ENTERTAINING THE
IDEA OF BEIN' A MOVIE STAR. MY
VARIETY SHOW, DOLLY, WAS BOR
THE SHOW OPENED EACH WEEK WITH A CLOSE-UP ON A BUTTERFLY MADE OF LIGHT PERCHED ATOP MY NAME. THE CAMERA WOULD PULL BACK, REVEALING MY NAME. I'D GLIDE INTO THE FRAME ON A VELVET ROPE SWING AS RALPH EMERY, OUR ANNOUNCER, SAID:
LADIES AND GENTLEMEN! MIS DOLLY PARTON
AND THEN I'D SING. IT WAS ALL VERY 1970'S.
THE SHOW WAS THE MOST EXPENSIVE SHOW EVER AIRED. IT COST $100,000 AN EPISODE AND ATTRACTED SINGERS LIKE EMMYLOU HARRIS, LINDA RONDSTADT, AND MARILYN MCCOO. IT WAS ALL REAL FANCY.
WE PULLED IN 9 MILLION VIEWERS A WEEK. NOT TOO SHABBY.
BUT IT WASN'T ENOUGH FOR ME. I PULLED THE PLUG AND THE STUDIO CITED IT AS "CREATIVE DIFFERENCES."

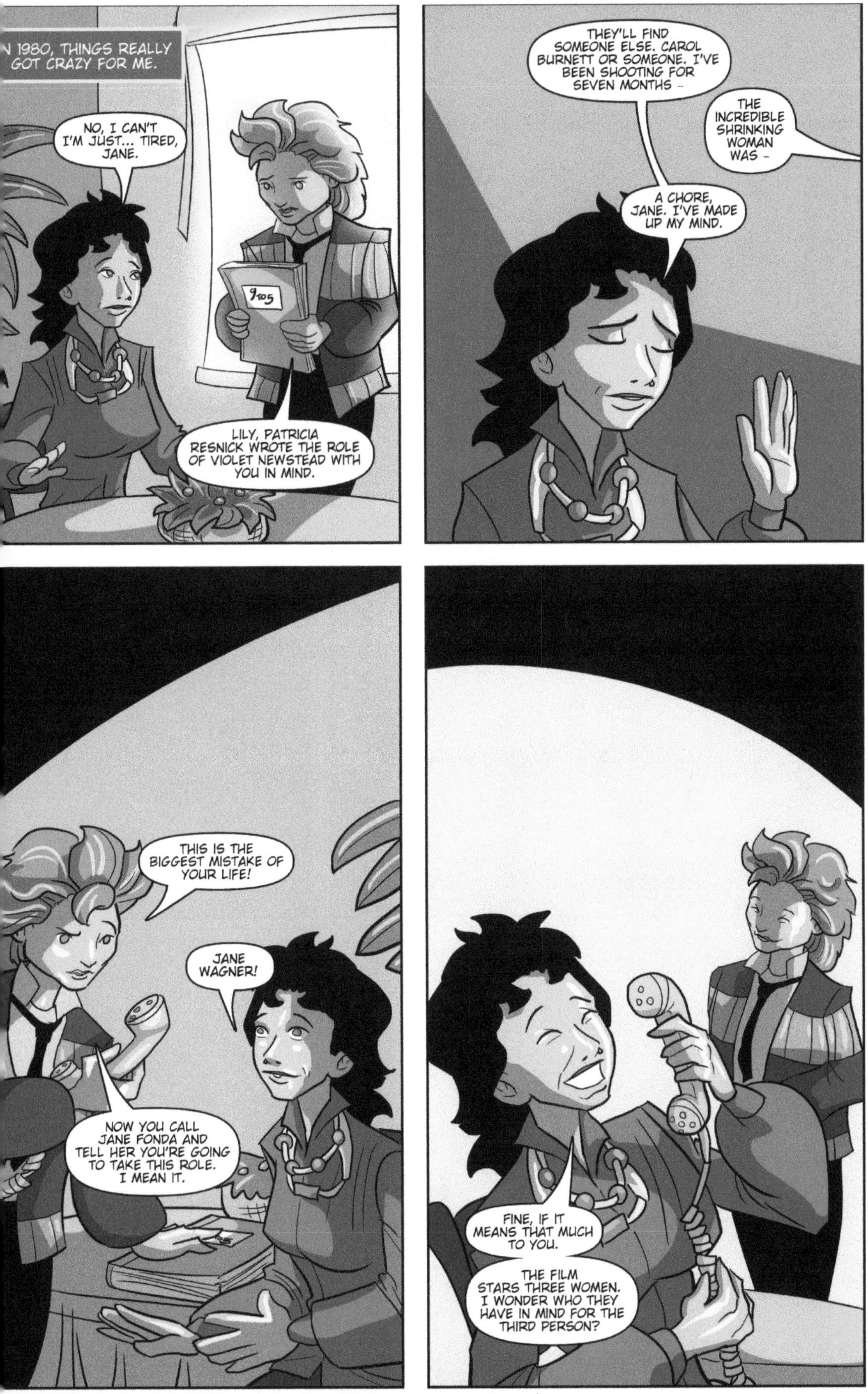
N 1980, THINGS REALLY GOT CRAZY FOR ME.
NO, I CAN'T I'M JUST... TIRED, JANE.
LILY, PATRICIA RESNICK WROTE THE ROLE OF VIOLET NEWSTEAD WITH YOU IN MIND.
THEY'LL FIND SOMEONE ELSE. CAROL BURNETT OR SOMEONE. I'VE BEEN SHOOTING FOR SEVEN MONTHS –
THE INCREDIBLE SHRINKING WOMAN WAS –
A CHORE, JANE. I'VE MADE UP MY MIND.
THIS IS THE BIGGEST MISTAKE OF YOUR LIFE!
JANE WAGNER!
NOW YOU CALL JANE FONDA AND TELL HER YOU'RE GOING TO TAKE THIS ROLE. I MEAN IT.
FINE, IF IT MEANS THAT MUCH TO YOU.
THE FILM STARS THREE WOMEN. I WONDER WHO THEY HAVE IN MIND FOR THE THIRD PERSON?

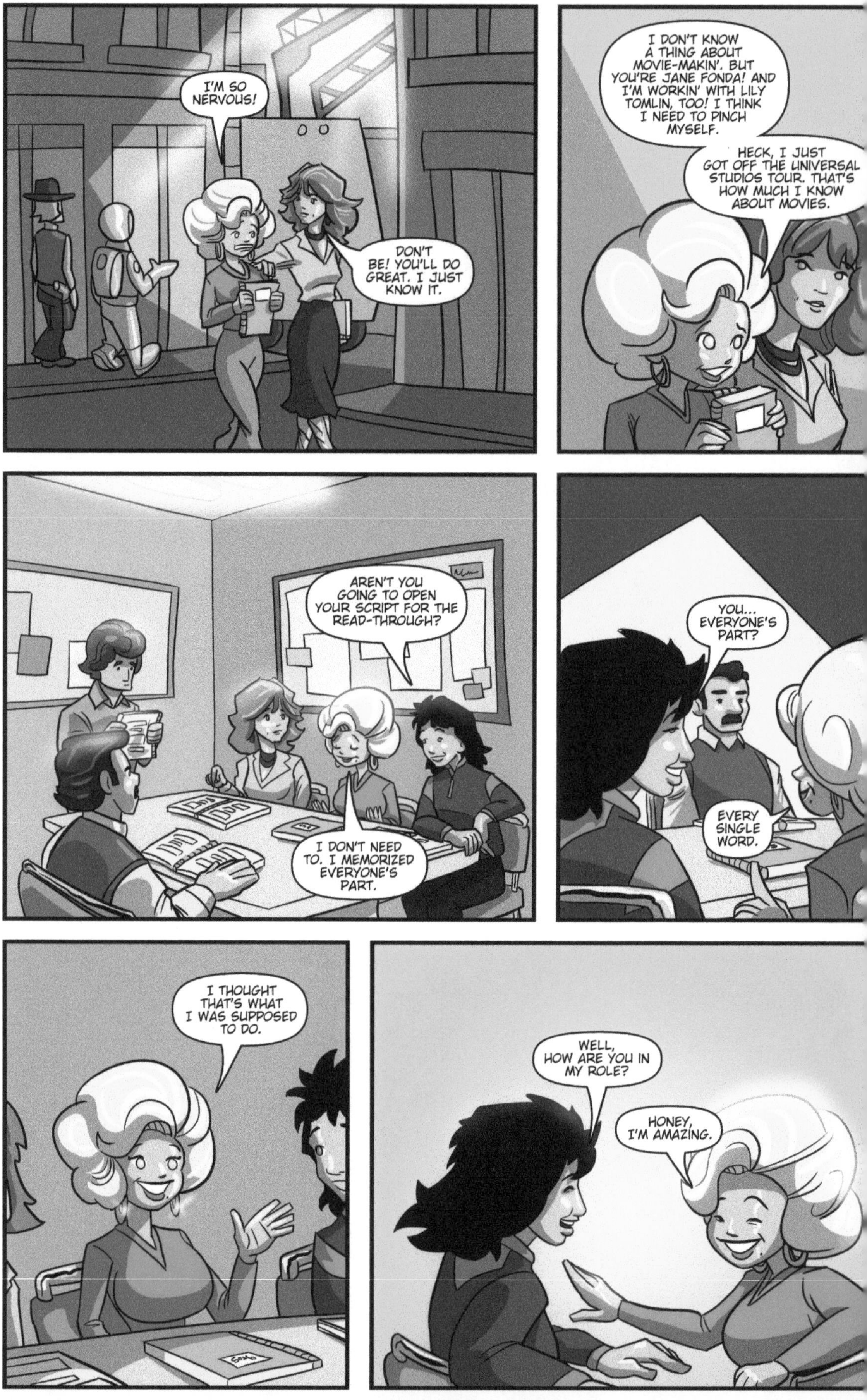
I'M SO NERVOUS!
DON'T BE! YOU'LL DO GREAT. I JUST KNOW IT.
I DON'T KNOW A THING ABOUT MOVIE-MAKIN'. BUT YOU'RE JANE FONDA! AND I'M WORKIN' WITH LILY TOMLIN, TOO! I THINK I NEED TO PINCH MYSELF.
HECK, I JUST GOT OFF THE UNIVERSAL STUDIOS TOUR. THAT'S HOW MUCH I KNOW ABOUT MOVIES.
AREN'T YOU GOING TO OPEN YOUR SCRIPT FOR THE READ-THROUGH?
I DON'T NEED TO. I MEMORIZED EVERYONE'S PART.
YOU... EVERYONE'S PART?
EVERY SINGLE WORD.
I THOUGHT THAT'S WHAT I WAS SUPPOSED TO DO.
WELL, HOW ARE YOU IN MY ROLE?
HONEY, I'M AMAZING.

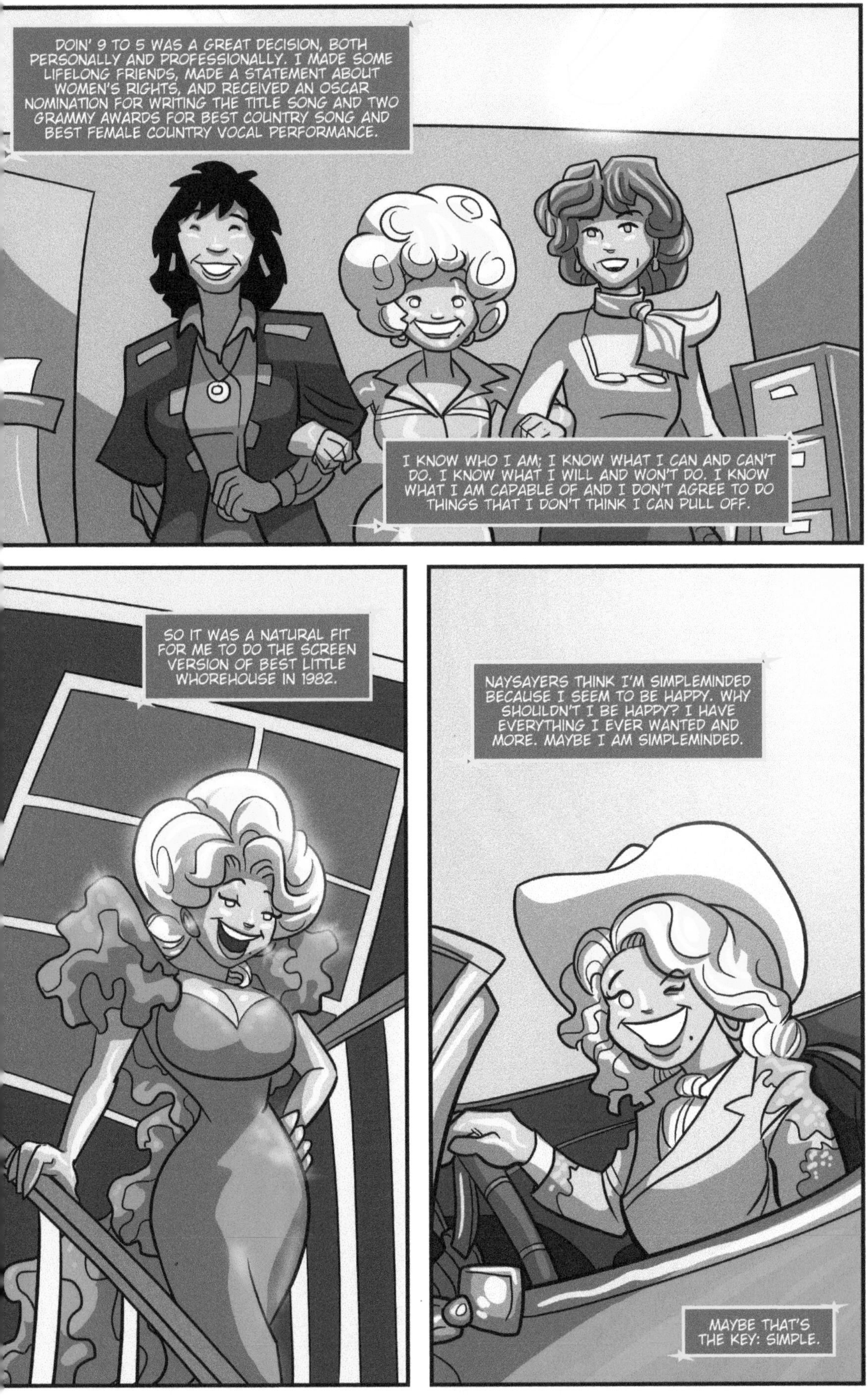
DOIN' 9 TO 5 WAS A GREAT DECISION, BOTH PERSONALLY AND PROFESSIONALLY. I MADE SOME LIFELONG FRIENDS, MADE A STATEMENT ABOUT WOMEN'S RIGHTS, AND RECEIVED AN OSCAR NOMINATION FOR WRITING THE TITLE SONG AND TWO GRAMMY AWARDS FOR BEST COUNTRY SONG AND BEST FEMALE COUNTRY VOCAL PERFORMANCE.
I KNOW WHO I AM; I KNOW WHAT I CAN AND CAN'T DO. I KNOW WHAT I WILL AND WON'T DO. I KNOW WHAT I AM CAPABLE OF AND I DON'T AGREE TO DO THINGS THAT I DON'T THINK I CAN PULL OFF.
SO IT WAS A NATURAL FIT FOR ME TO DO THE SCREEN VERSION OF BEST LITTLE WHOREHOUSE IN 1982.
NAYSAYERS THINK I'M SIMPLEMINDED BECAUSE I SEEM TO BE HAPPY. WHY SHOULDN'T I BE HAPPY? I HAVE EVERYTHING I EVER WANTED AND MORE. MAYBE I AM SIMPLEMINDED.
MAYBE THAT'S THE KEY: SIMPLE.

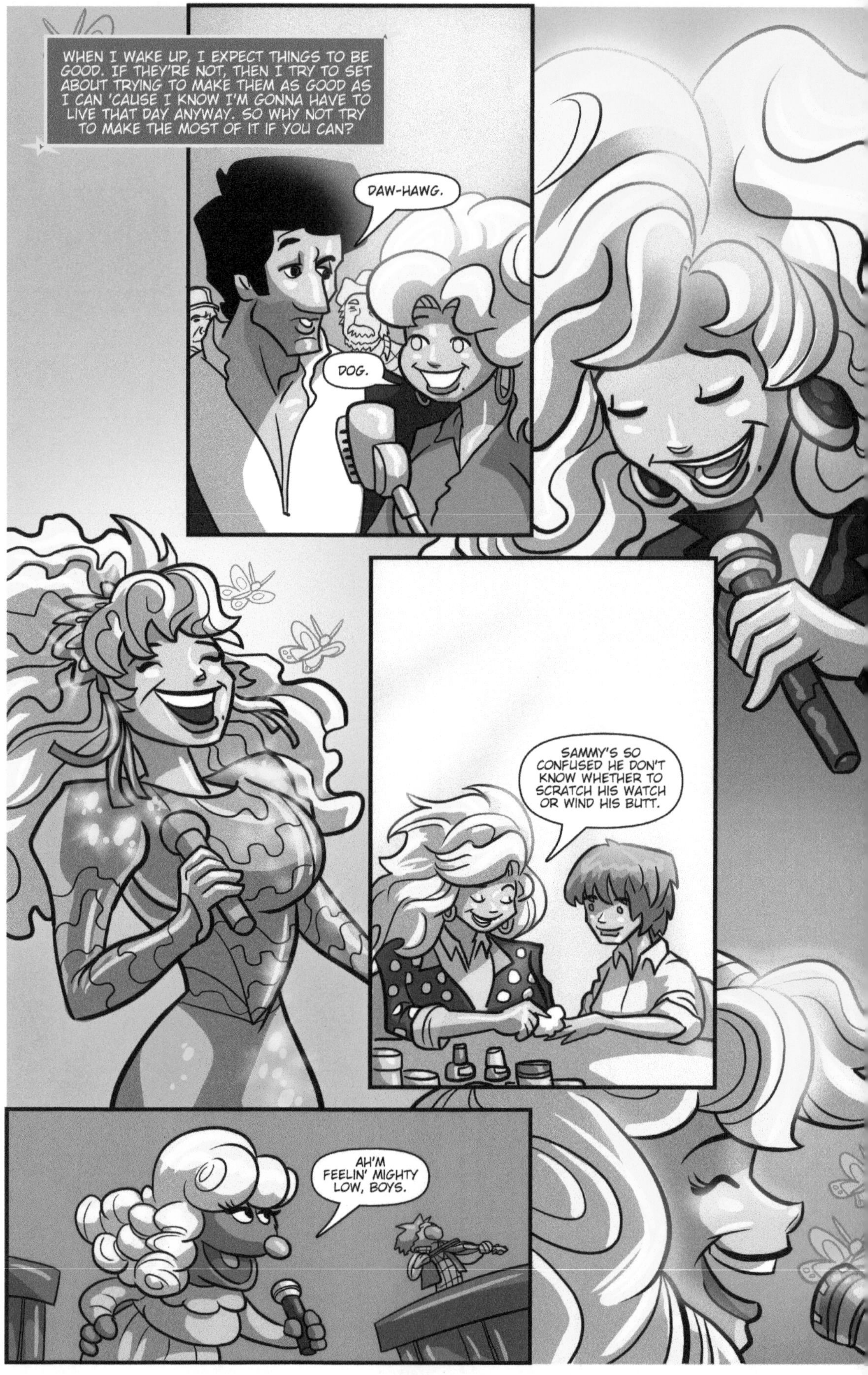
WHEN I WAKE UP, I EXPECT THINGS TO BE GOOD. IF THEY'RE NOT, THEN I TRY TO SET ABOUT TRYING TO MAKE THEM AS GOOD AS I CAN 'CAUSE I KNOW I'M GONNA HAVE TO LIVE THAT DAY ANYWAY. SO WHY NOT TRY TO MAKE THE MOST OF IT IF YOU CAN?
DAW-HAWG.
DOG.
SAMMY'S SO CONFUSED HE DON'T KNOW WHETHER TO SCRATCH HIS WATCH OR WIND HIS BUTT.
AH'M FEELIN' MIGHTY LOW, BOYS.

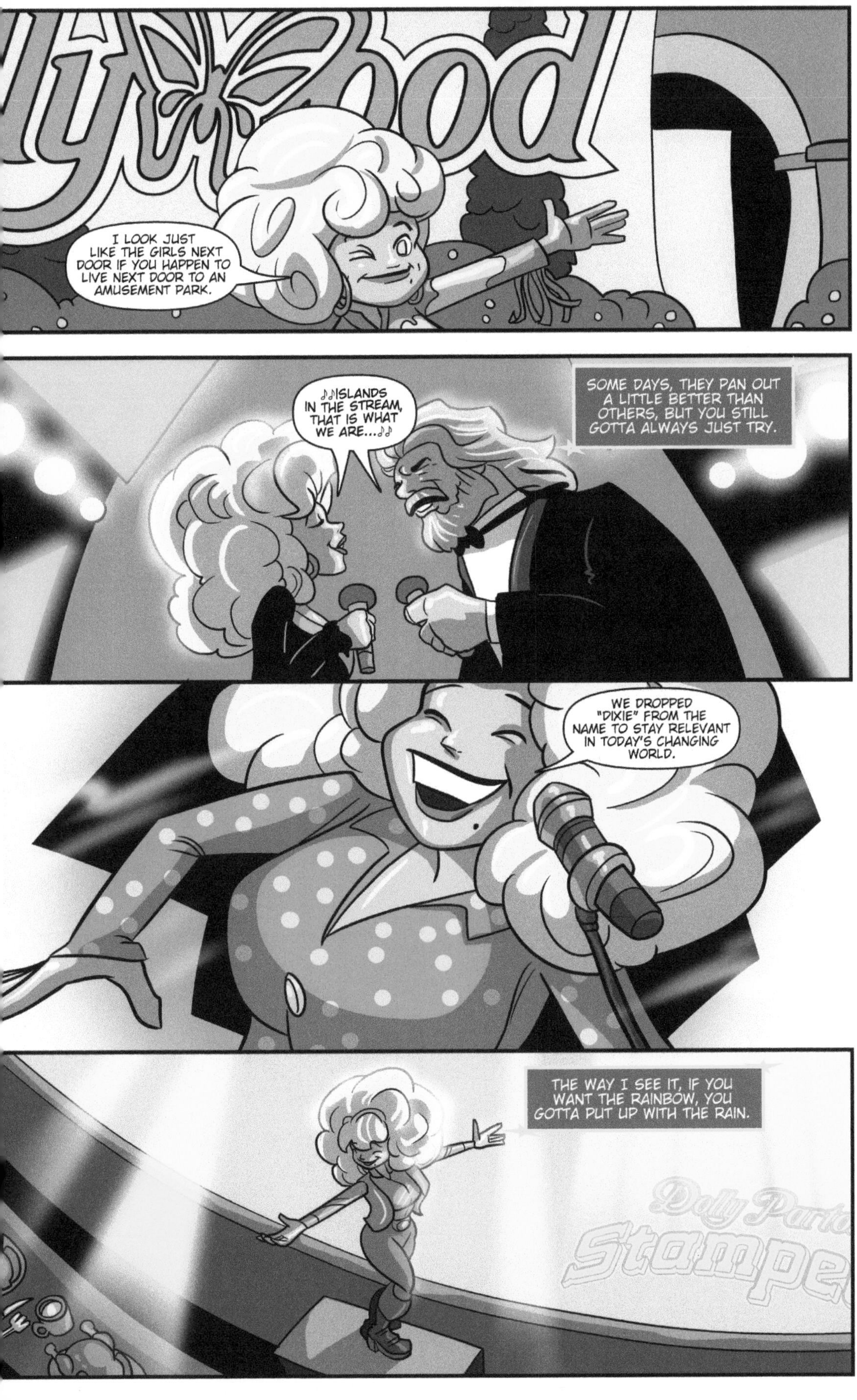

I LOOK JUST LIKE THE GIRLS NEXT DOOR IF YOU HAPPEN TO LIVE NEXT DOOR TO AN AMUSEMENT PARK.
♪♪ISLANDS IN THE STREAM, THAT IS WHAT WE ARE...♪♪
SOME DAYS, THEY PAN OUT A LITTLE BETTER THAN OTHERS, BUT YOU STILL GOTTA ALWAYS JUST TRY.
WE DROPPED "DIXIE" FROM THE NAME TO STAY RELEVANT IN TODAY'S CHANGING WORLD.
THE WAY I SEE IT, IF YOU WANT THE RAINBOW, YOU GOTTA PUT UP WITH THE RAIN.

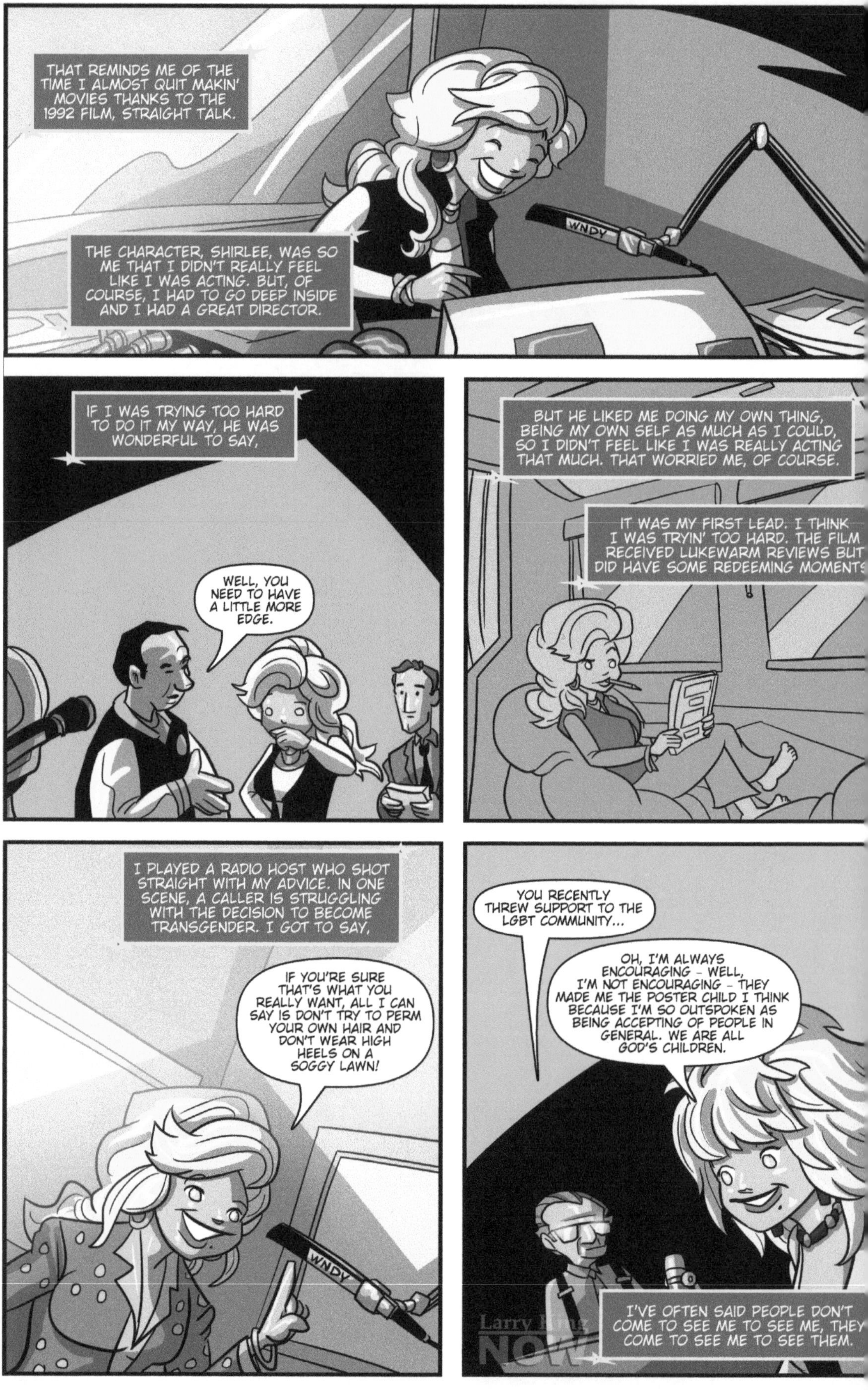
THAT REMINDS ME OF THE TIME I ALMOST QUIT MAKIN' MOVIES THANKS TO THE 1992 FILM, STRAIGHT TALK.
WNDY
THE CHARACTER, SHIRLEE, WAS SO ME THAT I DIDN'T REALLY FEEL LIKE I WAS ACTING. BUT, OF COURSE, I HAD TO GO DEEP INSIDE AND I HAD A GREAT DIRECTOR.
IF I WAS TRYING TOO HARD TO DO IT MY WAY, HE WAS WONDERFUL TO SAY,
WELL, YOU NEED TO HAVE A LITTLE MORE EDGE.
BUT HE LIKED ME DOING MY OWN THING, BEING MY OWN SELF AS MUCH AS I COULD, SO I DIDN'T FEEL LIKE I WAS REALLY ACTING THAT MUCH. THAT WORRIED ME, OF COURSE.
IT WAS MY FIRST LEAD. I THINK I WAS TRYIN' TOO HARD. THE FILM RECEIVED LUKEWARM REVIEWS BUT DID HAVE SOME REDEEMING MOMENTS.
I PLAYED A RADIO HOST WHO SHOT STRAIGHT WITH MY ADVICE. IN ONE SCENE, A CALLER IS STRUGGLING WITH THE DECISION TO BECOME TRANSGENDER. I GOT TO SAY,
IF YOU'RE SURE THAT'S WHAT YOU REALLY WANT, ALL I CAN SAY IS DON'T TRY TO PERM YOUR OWN HAIR AND DON'T WEAR HIGH HEELS ON A SOGGY LAWN!
WNDY
YOU RECENTLY THREW SUPPORT TO THE LGBT COMMUNITY...
OH, I'M ALWAYS ENCOURAGING - WELL, I'M NOT ENCOURAGING - THEY MADE ME THE POSTER CHILD I THINK BECAUSE I'M SO OUTSPOKEN AS BEING ACCEPTING OF PEOPLE IN GENERAL. WE ARE ALL GOD'S CHILDREN.
I'VE OFTEN SAID PEOPLE DON'T COME TO SEE ME TO SEE ME, THEY COME TO SEE ME TO SEE THEM.

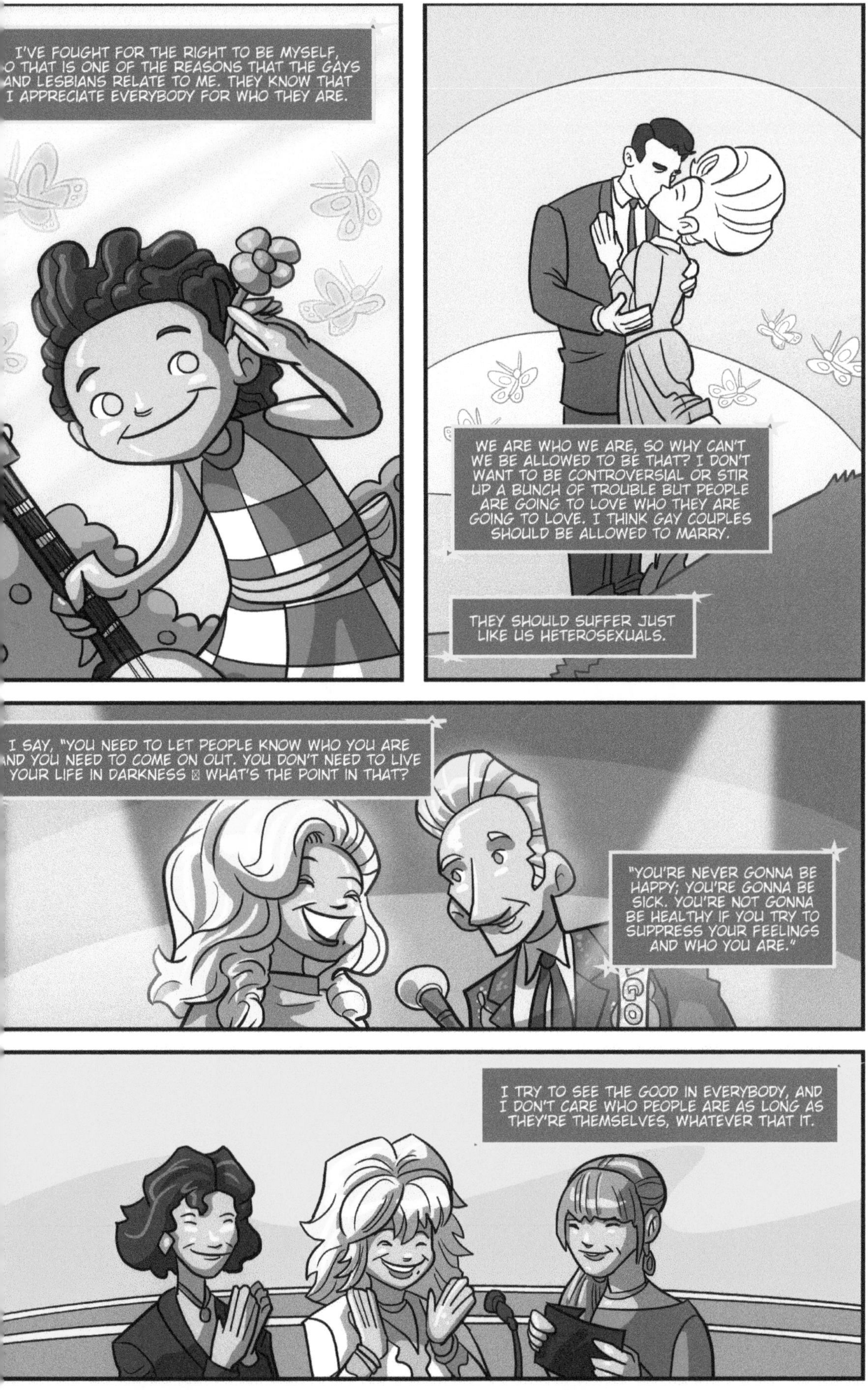
I'VE FOUGHT FOR THE RIGHT TO BE MYSELF, O THAT IS ONE OF THE REASONS THAT THE GAYS AND LESBIANS RELATE TO ME. THEY KNOW THAT I APPRECIATE EVERYBODY FOR WHO THEY ARE.
WE ARE WHO WE ARE, SO WHY CAN'T WE BE ALLOWED TO BE THAT? I DON'T WANT TO BE CONTROVERSIAL OR STIR UP A BUNCH OF TROUBLE BUT PEOPLE ARE GOING TO LOVE WHO THEY ARE GOING TO LOVE. I THINK GAY COUPLES SHOULD BE ALLOWED TO MARRY.
THEY SHOULD SUFFER JUST LIKE US HETEROSEXUALS.
I SAY, "YOU NEED TO LET PEOPLE KNOW WHO YOU ARE ND YOU NEED TO COME ON OUT. YOU DON'T NEED TO LIVE YOUR LIFE IN DARKNESS ⊠ WHAT'S THE POINT IN THAT?
"YOU'RE NEVER GONNA BE HAPPY; YOU'RE GONNA BE SICK. YOU'RE NOT GONNA BE HEALTHY IF YOU TRY TO SUPPRESS YOUR FEELINGS AND WHO YOU ARE."
I TRY TO SEE THE GOOD IN EVERYBODY, AND I DON'T CARE WHO PEOPLE ARE AS LONG AS THEY'RE THEMSELVES, WHATEVER THAT IT.

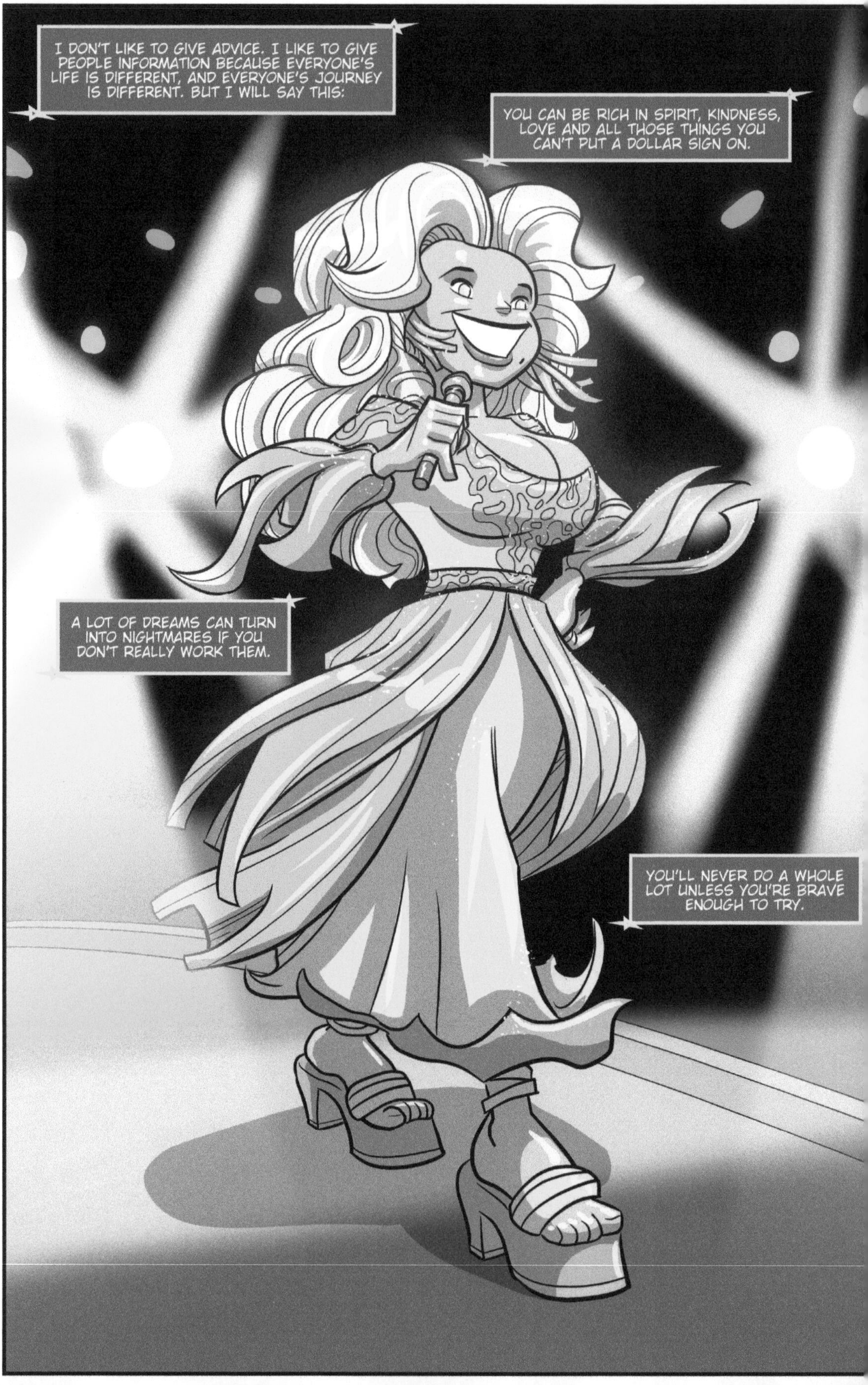
I DON'T LIKE TO GIVE ADVICE. I LIKE TO GIVE PEOPLE INFORMATION BECAUSE EVERYONE'S LIFE IS DIFFERENT, AND EVERYONE'S JOURNEY IS DIFFERENT. BUT I WILL SAY THIS:
YOU CAN BE RICH IN SPIRIT, KINDNESS, LOVE AND ALL THOSE THINGS YOU CAN'T PUT A DOLLAR SIGN ON.
A LOT OF DREAMS CAN TURN INTO NIGHTMARES IF YOU DON'T REALLY WORK THEM.
YOU'LL NEVER DO A WHOLE LOT UNLESS YOU'RE BRAVE ENOUGH TO TRY.

TIDALWAVE
COMICS

Michael Frizell — Writer

Ramon Salas — Art

Benjamin Glibert — Letters

Darren G. Davis — Editor

Dave Ryan — Cover

Cover B: Ramon Salas

Darren G. Davis
Publisher

Maggie Jessup
Publicity

Susan Ferris
Entertainment Manager

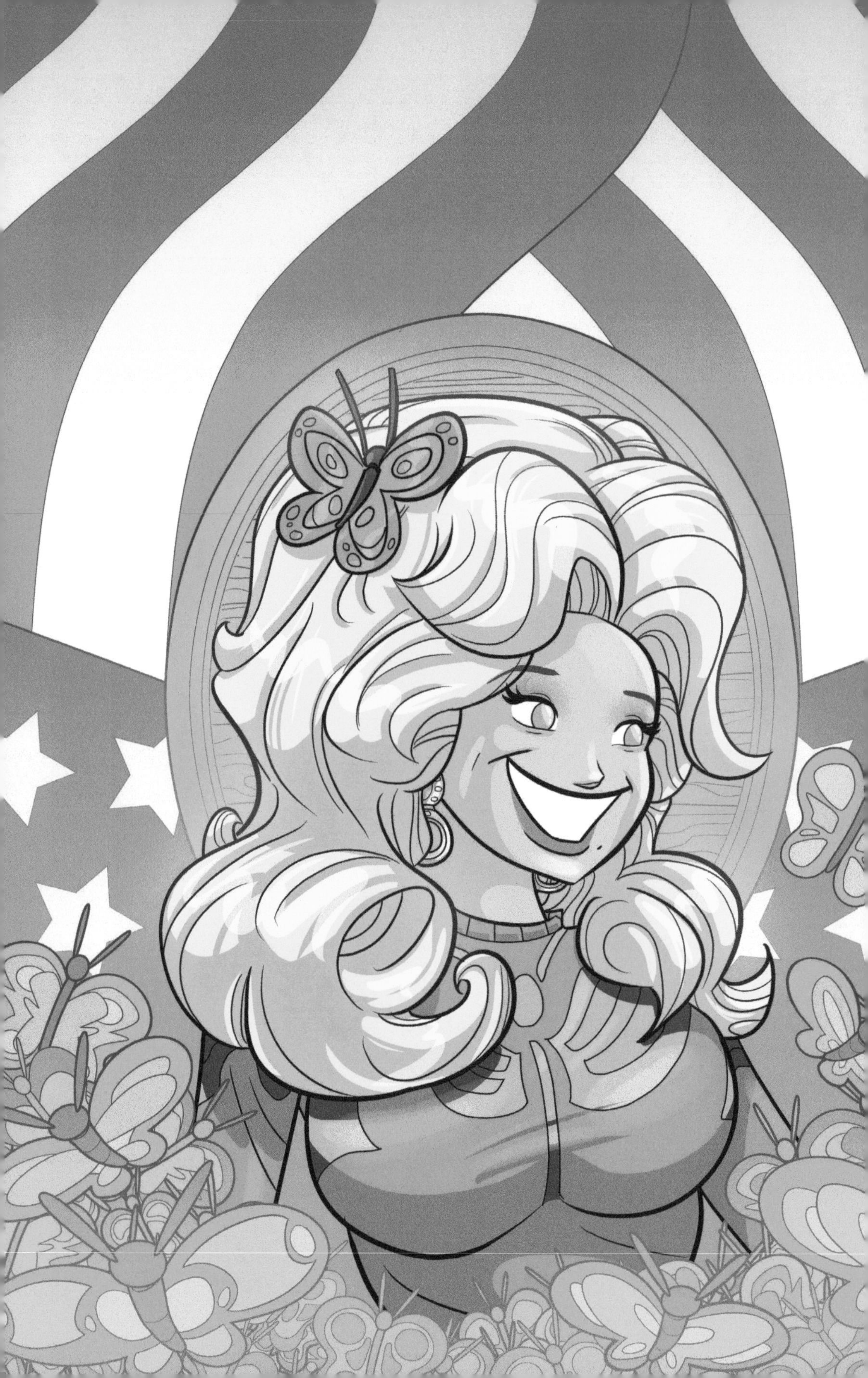

CPSIA information can be obtained
at www.ICGtesting.com
Printed in the USA
LVHW072355290321
682890LV00031B/1193

9 781954 044500